Learn About
NEPTUNE!

BY DANIELLE HAYNES

Enslow
PUBLISHING

DISCOVER!

Please visit our website, www.enslow.com. For a free color catalog of all our high-quality books, call toll free 1-800-398-2504 or fax 1-877-980-4454.

Cataloging-in-Publication Data

Names: Haynes, Danielle.
Title: Learn about Neptune! / Danielle Haynes.
Description: New York : Enslow Publishing, 2024. | Series: Planets in our solar system | Includes index.
Identifiers: ISBN 9781978533615 (pbk.) | ISBN 9781978533622 (library bound) | ISBN 9781978533639 (ebook)
Subjects: LCSH: Neptune (Planet)–Juvenile literature.
Classification: LCC QB691.H394 2024 | DDC 523.48–dc23

Portions of this work were originally authored by Greg Roza and published as *Neptune: The Stormy Planet*. All new material in this edition authored by Danielle Haynes.

Published in 2024 by
Enslow Publishing
2544 Clinton Street
Buffalo, NY 14224

Designer: Andrea Davison-Bartolotta
Editor: Danielle Haynes

Photo credits: Cover (Neptune), p. 1 (Neptune) 24K-Production/Shutterstock.com; cover (top), p. 1 (top), series art (backgrounds) Jurik Peter/Shutterstock.com; series art (lens flare) andruxevich/Shutterstock.com; p. 4 Natee Jitthammachai/Shutterstock.com; p. 5 (both) Vadim Sadovski/Shutterstock.com; p. 6 HAKAN AKIRMAK VISUALS/Shutterstock.com; p. 7 Devotion/Shutterstock.com; pp. 8, 19 NASA/JPL; p. 9 courtesy of NASA; p. 11 vikas31/Shutterstock.com; p. 13 K.K.T Madhusanka/Shutterstock.com; p. 14 buradaki/Shutterstock.com; pp. 15, 17 Tristan3D/Shutterstock.com; p. 21 NASA, ESA, CSA, STScI.

Printed in the United States of America

CPSIA compliance information: Batch #CS24ENS: For further information contact Enslow Publishing, at 1-800-398-2504.

Find us on

CONTENTS

Boldface words appear in Words to Know.

Neptune is the eighth planet in our **solar system**. It's the farthest planet away from the sun—more than 30 times as far as the Earth! It's so far away that humans need a **telescope** to see it.

NEPTUNE

PLUTO

Pluto used to be the farthest planet from the sun, but scientists decided it wasn't a planet in 2006.

Neptune takes a long time to **orbit** the sun. It takes about 165 Earth years to orbit just once! On July 12, 2011, Neptune finished its first full orbit since it was discovered in 1846.

Sometimes Neptune's orbit takes it farther away from the sun than Pluto.

URANUS

MERCURY SUN

EARTH

Neptune is called a gas giant. It's **surrounded** by clouds. The **atmosphere** is very windy on Neptune. Below the clouds is a thick **layer** of gases. It doesn't have solid ground like Earth does.

CLOUDS ON NEPTUNE

Because Neptune doesn't have a
solid surface, no person could ever
walk on it like they do on Earth.

Different parts of Neptune spin at different speeds. This is because it is not solid. The middle part makes one full spin about every 18 hours. The top and bottom parts can make one full spin in just 12 hours.

1 SPIN EVERY 12 HOURS

1 SPIN EVERY 18 HOURS

1 SPIN EVERY 12 HOURS

One "day" on Neptune lasts about 16 hours.

Neptune's atmosphere is made mostly of gases. The blue color comes from the gas **methane**. The next layer is water and melted ice. Neptune's center, or core, is made of ice and rock. Its core is about the size of Earth!

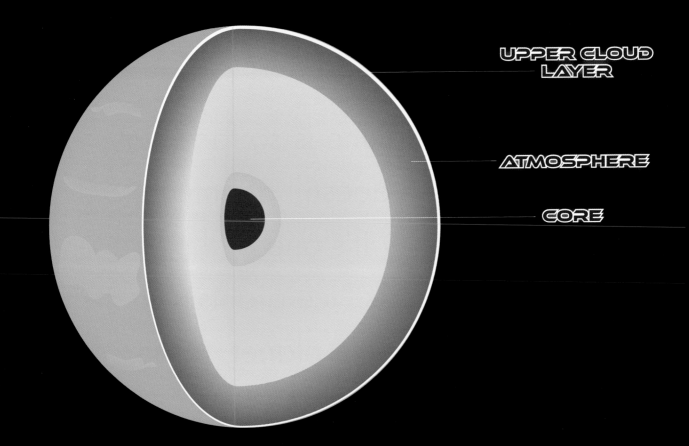

UPPER CLOUD LAYER

ATMOSPHERE

CORE

Winds on Neptune can make the gas methane layer move at speeds of more than 1,200 miles (2,000 km) per hour.

Because Neptune is so far away from the sun, it doesn't get much heat. That's why it's one of the two planets known as "ice giants." Uranus, the seventh planet, is the other ice giant.

NEPTUNE

URANUS

Uranus and Neptune look alike. Uranus is a lighter blue, while Neptune's atmosphere has storm spots.

Getting STORMY

Neptune is a very stormy planet. Sometimes Neptune has dark spots on it. These dark spots are huge storms. They have very strong winds. Neptune has the fastest winds in our solar system. The planet's winds are about nine times faster than winds on Earth!

GREAT DARK SPOT

In 1989, Neptune formed a huge spot called the "Great Dark Spot." It was big enough to fit all of Earth inside it.

Scientists sent a **probe** called Voyager 2 to study Neptune. Voyager 2 passed by Neptune in 1989. The probe found five moons. The largest moon is named Triton. Since then, more moons have been found. The Hubble Space Telescope found a 14th moon in 2013.

Scientists first discovered Triton in 1846. The moon's atmosphere is growing warmer, but scientists don't know why.

Voyager 2 also showed scientists that Neptune has rings like Saturn. Neptune's rings are not as thick as Saturn's rings. This makes them harder to see. The James Webb Space Telescope sent into space in 2021 saw the rings for the first time in 30 years!

The James Webb Space Telescope takes pictures of planets and stars from space.

WORDS TO KNOW

atmosphere: The mixture of gases that surround a planet.

layer: One thickness of something lying over or under another.

methane: A common gas in the solar system. On Earth, it is found in natural gas.

orbit: To travel in a circle or oval around something, or the path used to make that trip.

probe: An unmanned spaceship.

solar system: The sun and all the space objects that orbit it, including the planets and their moons.

surround: To have something in the space all around an object.

telescope: A tool used to make faraway objects look bigger and closer.

FOR MORE INFORMATION

BOOKS

Foxe, Steve. *Neptune*. North Mankato, MN: Pebble, 2021.

Gater, Will. *The Mysteries of the Universe*. New York, NY: DK Publishing, 2020.

WEBSITES

All About Neptune

spaceplace.nasa.gov/all-about-neptune/en/
Learn about Neptune with the help of photos and fact boxes.

National Air and Space Museum

airandspace.si.edu/
This website teaches all about the history of flight and space in the United States.

INDEX